AN OTHER PERSPECTIVE

A Guide For Living Well

Heikkie Dean

To order additional copies of this book, contact:
Xlibris Corporation
1-888-795-4274
www.Xlibris.com
Orders@Xlibris.com
25622

Heikkie Dean is a counselor working in a post Jungian modality in San Francisco. For the past 3 decades he has helped others to change and grow. He has often said that he wants to be a true being in every sense of the word.

INTRODUCTION

Thank you for buying this book.

In buying this book you have made another investment in yourself. Any time you use money, power, or time you are making an investment in yourself. It's a very simple concept with far-reaching consequences. Life is like that. Money, power and time will feature prominently in this book, as will the issue of self-love, also known as self-esteem. And let's start with investment opportunities,

Such as a class or seminar you attend.
Like clothes or food or anything you buy.
Or a friendship or an acquaintance or a marriage.
A walk in the woods.

Your investment in this book can change your life, not just your income or your image or your waist size or your relationships. With the knowledge this book contains, you will have the single most important element you need in order to make your life however you choose. That element is an authentic YOU.

CHANGE

Change is constant, whether we admit it or not.

Time, that most precious and fleeting of gifts, is both the boon of man's existence and the source of his greatest dread. Few of us know in our own heart or mind the exact moment of our death, but we do have the gift of memory.

Yesterday does not need to be the blueprint for today.

We can embark on each new day as a new beginning.

With these ideas in mind, I wrote this book to share ideas and concepts that have helped to make my life flow well. It is my prayer that it does the same for you.

For this book to have its greatest impact on you please follow the instructions as they are given. And do try the exercises. They are there to help you.

IN THE BEGINNING

Inviting transformation into your life. That's what this book is all about.

I wrote this book to help those who are ready for an improvement in their lives—to help them clarify those issues that are troublesome to them and to share my experiences to help find solutions to any outstanding problems and conflicts that may be holding back that improvement.

Transformation, which also goes by the word change, is an ongoing process. It is a process that gives you the freedom and ability to alter your life to reflect your true desires and to truly portray yourself as you would like to be and can become.

It is not a perfect world, at least not yet. But being part of the problem, being part of that imperfection, is a choice we make.

There are many differing examples of "how to be" in this world. Some people choose to be happy, some choose to be sad. Some choose to feel superior, while others choose to feel inferior. There are countless choices of how to be.

No one makes you choose your feelings.

You choose, all the time.

Let's look at an example:

At one time or another, most of us have said, "(blank) makes me feel so. . . ."

In reality, though, no other person can reach inside us and adjust an imaginary set of controls to some certain setting, some way of expressing our emotions. When we say that something or someone is responsible for how and what we feel, we deny our own responsibility for what our feelings are.

When we do this, we remove ourselves from any position of power. We become the victim.

That is the choice we make.

We choose.
All the time.

Life is not a matter of whether we choose, but what we choose. Our choices in life can, and will, have profound effects on the very nature and quality of the lives we live.

This book will ask you to explore some, and perhaps all, of the choices you have made in your life.

It will ask you to examine your language and speech, your sense of self, your fears and worries and shames.

The process of true change involves work. Hard work. This book will ask you to work for you and to make your life better for you.

Take a deep breath.

Breathe.

Do it again.

Loosen or take off your shoes.

Relax.

Get truly and honestly comfortable.

Congratulations!

I f you have followed the instructions on the preceding pages, you have done a good thing for you.

If you have not followed them, then you have chosen not to follow them. Does your decision feel good, in your head and heart?

You can choose again. It is always your choice.

Give yourself permission to follow the directions in this book.

We make choices all the time. Sometimes we will jump right in there and deride our actions. We even second-guess ourselves and others. When we do this, we are making a negative choice.

A negative choice does not encourage us. A negative choice does not empower us, but it does reflect a base-line, if you will, exposing our current psycho-emotional frame of being, of living.

This emotional frame of mind is mirrored in our life.

Many people have asked me why their lives are as they are. For the most part the answer is always the same, in that they do not change. How can one expect life to change if one is not willing to change? It really is just that simple.

Choose to change for the better.

EXERCISE ONE

The purpose of this exercise is to start a reckoning of our self at our worst.

To accomplish this do the following:

At the back of this book are blank pages for you to use to accomplish some of the exercises in this book. Take one of these pages and something to write with. Write down the answers to these questions:

What are the meanest things you say to yourself?
When do you say them?

Do this now.

When you have finished writing down your answers, set your writing aside. Put it somewhere no one will read what you've written, and where you feel safe about putting it. Leave it there at least overnight.

When you are ready, go to a place that feels good to you, be there by yourself, and read your writing out loud.

When you've finished reading your writing out loud, take a breath. Let your feelings come up. If it feels comfortable to you, give voice and action to your feelings.

The point of the foregoing exercise is to use a physical action to transform those deep, dark, ugly thoughts into something concrete and then to change that something concrete into yet another thing.

By bringing together our memories of pain and hurt, our intellectual and emotional responses, we can then use the body to release the joining together of these memories and responses. This process is called conjunctive energy displacement.

It is fundamental to wellness and well-being.

We will be stuck with part, if not all, of our negative thoughts and emotions and memories unless we displace them. In time, this will lead to depression and disease. When we do displace our negative thoughts and emotions and memories, we replace them with wellness. Wellness leads to joy. Wellness and happiness lie in being as free from negative energy as possible. This means some work on one's part, to be sure, but consider the trade-off.

Repeated acts of the exercise just completed can lead to sustained wellness.

And eventually to sustained joy.

Most of us just stuff our feelings, having been conditioned by a lifetime of experiences of stuffing our feelings, maybe to not draw negative attention, perhaps to gain approval, but the message is always the same: do not express yourself honestly.

Societal forces also play a major part in influencing how we act, how we appear. Most of us know of someone who suppresses their feelings and are aware when we suppress our own feelings. The suppression comes easily after time, as we repeat the repression technique that is unique to us, the control mechanism, if you will, that becomes our methodology of self control.

What a way to live . . .

E instein said that energy is matter. E=MC squared. A scientific basis for life. So where does emotional energy go once it is created?

If I get really angry, where does the energy go?

I remember once seeing a man walking across the floor of a terminal at New York's LaGuardia Airport just as he slipped and fell. His briefcase hit the floor so hard it popped open and sprayed its contents allover the floor. A porter helped the man to his feet and helped him pick up his stuff. The man thanked the porter, went over to a phone and called someone. He stood there talking, and a short while later I heard him shouting into the telephone. As I watched he then slammed down the receiver and stormed off. He was so angry his face was bright red.

What happens to the emotional energy that was that man's anger?

Where does it go? If Einstein is right, that energy is matter, then the energy is still present. Since the only "matter," or physical form, present was that man, I believe the energy stayed in him and lit up his being, so to speak. It turned his face a bright red. I also believe that his yelling into the phone, rightly or wrongly, helped him to displace some of the anger that he felt. It did not displace all of his anger because he slammed down the receiver and stormed away from the phone obviously very angry and upset.

Once energy has been created, it must be dissipated or directed outwards. Otherwise it stays with one and doesn't go anywhere.

Undissipated emotional energy stays with us and binds with the structure of our bodies. Undissipated emotional energy affects how we look, how we feel, how long we live, and the quality of our lives. I believe it is the cause of dis-ease, and is at the root of most physical illnesses.

EXERCISE TWO

The purpose of this exercise is to reconnect with long buried, and perhaps forgotten, emotions that are at the base of today's problems. To accomplish this, do the following:

Make photocopies of several photographs of yourself taken when you were a child, preferably under the age of eight years old.

On the back of each copy write out your memories and associated negative emotions as they relate to each photograph copy. Be thorough and honest. If you have to use them, keep the rationalizations to a minimum. Purge yourself of any stored negative feelings connected with the photographs. Be as emotional in your writing as you wish. Write down the emotions that you feel.

As you did with Exercise One, put this writing away in a safe place where no one will see it. Leave it there until you are ready for the next step.

When you are ready, go to a nice place and dispose of the writing in the way that you think is best and most correct.

The purpose of this exercise is to get rid of stored negative energies of our feelings and memories by using photographs to help recall those negative feelings and our memories.

Photographs are powerful tools, especially when they are used as aids to help to bring up buried negative emotions, feelings and memories. For the past 20 years I have had great success using old photographs of one's relatives to purge stored negative energy and help people move on with their lives.

STARTING ON THE PATH

As I look back over the lunar-Iike landscape of my life, one immense fact strikes home: the quality of my life is in direct proportion to the amount of positive self-esteem I have felt at a given time.

When I have felt terrible about myself, the quality of my life has been terrible. When I felt good, life was good. When I felt badly, those things that I enjoyed doing usually helped me to feel better about myself.

So I indulged myself and told myself that it was all right to do whatever it was that helped me feel better. Then I used those indulgences as a crutch to get through rough spots in my days. What sort of indulgence was it? Just about anything. It could be food, money, sex or whatever. They all produced pleasurable feelings in me and voila! I had instant relief from my pain. It was just like I had a magic way to find relief. Temporary relief, to be sure, but relief nonetheless.

What was really happening? What I really was doing was escaping my pain by indulging in certain pleasures, certain external acts, in an effort to feel better about myself. But I was just escaping my pain. I wasn't really resolving my pain. I wasn't building self-esteem.

Escapism is not authentic self-esteem. Feeling good about one's self because of some external act or thing is a starting point, but it's only a starting point. At the same time it can leave one at the mercy of the external, which is not good. Here are a few examples of people using external acts to escape internal pain.

A woman I know of racked up nearly $100,000 in credit card debt, all because she was depressed most of the time. Things got so bad that the telephone clerks at a TV home shopping program began to recognize her voice and call her by name. She felt better about herself whenever she bought something, so she kept on shopping. She didn't realize that what she was doing was escaping her depression, not healing it. She continued to shop and charge purchases to her credit cards until she was nearly bankrupt. Finally, she sought help.

She acknowledged that her shopping was a means of escaping her depression rather than confronting it head-on and working to heal it. She stopped shopping. She worked hard to truly heal her depression. She resolved her credit card debt. She healed her depression. It took time and hard work, but today she is debt free.

A man I know of used to have sex with strangers to help him feel better about himself. It didn't matter who his partner was or what time of day it was, so long as the result was that he felt better about himself afterward. He never told his wife what he was doing. His children knew nothing about it, of course. He continued this activity until one day when his wife and children spotted him getting out of his car with a transvestite companion.

Being seen this way by those so close to him shocked him into recognizing that what he was doing was hurting his family and not really helping him, so he sought to help himself. In time he came to realize that his "relief" was only a temporary escape. He wanted to feel better about himself permanently. He worked long and hard to feel genuinely better about himself, to restore his self-esteem if you will, without resorting to having potentially self-destructive sex with strangers. He made peace with his wife and children. Today they are reunited as a family and living together happily.

I used to chat with a politician who was then a heavy cocaine user. He used the drug to feel better about himself. He knew that the feeling he got from using the drug was temporary, but to feel good about himself, even temporarily, was better than feeling poorly about himself. He had a serious cocaine habit that he would not give up. He lied to his friends about it and kept it secret from just about everyone. He and I would discuss how this habit would one day jeopardize his whole life and his career if he didn't change. He was right. He did put his life and career in jeopardy. He continued to use the drug until finally, one day he realized what he had done and kept on doing. He was on a downward slide.

As part of delegation at the opening of a new drug treatment center in his town he talked with one of the attendees. The man told him how he had been happy and successful prior to his alcohol abuse and what happened because of it. As the politician listened he heard his story coming out of the man, and recognized that the gulf between them was an illusion. He broke down and sobbed.

He became honest about his problem and shared his story with counselors and treatment professionals. He struggled to give up drugs. He worked really hard to stop. He succeeded. Today he is drug free. His life and career are back on track.

These are good examples of people turning their lives around. Of people working hard to move from escaping their difficulties to healing them and regaining their self-esteem.

Self-esteem is another name for how we feel about ourselves. How we live our lives is a direct reflection of how we feel about ourselves, of how high or low our self-esteem is at any given point in time. If our lives are in the gutter it is because that is where we (yes, I mean you and me and every other human being) think they ought to be. Remarkably, this is true whether or not we realize what our thoughts are about where we feel our lives should be.

I used to believe in fate. I believed that some one or some agency was determining what would happen in my life and that it was up to me to figure out how to handle what "they" decided my life would be.

I used to believe in negative reincarnation. What that means is that I believed that when bad things happened to me it was because I had been bad once before, maybe in another life, and that that was why I was being punished now—to atone for the wrongs I had done earlier, not necessarily during my current lifetime. "Earlier" could go as far back as the beginning of time.

For years and years I have searched for the answer as to why things—good things and bad things, but particularly bad things—

happened to me and how it happened to be me that they happened to. What I have come to see, to realize, is that how I feel about myself in large part determines how my life will proceed. If I feel good about myself and my life, my life will be happy and good. Conversely, if I walk around with a negative attitude and poor feelings about my life, then my life will soon resemble what I perceive as "my lot in life," something out of my control.

The nearly bankrupt woman shopper I mentioned was confusing feeling better about herself with spending money on nice new things. She believed that by investing in clothing she was investing in herself, and that appearance in life was more important than how she felt to be alive. Which made each day harder than the next. When she saw most of her clothes burn in a fire she quickly realized the difference between her self and her stuff, her possessions.

The man who had sex with strangers "got it" when he looked into his children's eyes and saw only love and admiration even as he stood before them in a terrible moment. He got honest about his emotional needs. It was hard on him and on his wife, but they worked it out together. They pulled through and today they are happier than ever before.

The cocaine-sniffing politician got out of politics, kicked his habit and today he runs a nice little non-profit organization that helps the general populace.

Each of these folks changed because they chose to change. They worked at it. Day by day, night by night, in real time. They did what it took to make their lives work. Each of them invited change into their lives. And change they did.

I know that all of them agree that they have changed for the better and that their lives have improved because of their hard work and the changes they have made.

If you walk around telling yourself how bad or stupid or awful you are, what you are really doing is beating yourself up. This does not invite change into your life. Worse, you may convince yourself that you really are bad or stupid or awful.

The shopper, the unfaithful husband and the politician were all beating themselves up. They were just using shopping, sex and cocaine to beat themselves up in addition to the thoughts in their heads.

Telling yourself how bad or stupid or awful you are only reinforces the bad and painful elements of your life. And when you reinforce the bad and the painful parts, what happens to the good and the happy elements of your life?

Isn't it possible that continually reinforcing the bad and the painful can eventually wipe out the good and the happy? Wouldn't the other way around make for a happier you? Reinforcing the bad does not help us in any positive way.

Look at it this way: if beating ourselves up made us into better persons, we'd all be close to perfect by now. The last I checked, we were still a ways from perfect. And life is not about being perfect without being happy.

EXERCISE THREE

The purpose of this exercise is for you to try to begin to understand how your thoughts and actions manifest themselves in your life and can become self-fulfilling prophecies.

This exercise requires what I call "self compassion." What that means is that you sympathize with yourself, that is, you are sympathetic to your own distress and at the same time to have a genuine desire to alleviate that distress.

Self-compassion also means to take care of you, in the most literal sense. When you are taking care of yourself, you take care of that part of the terrain entrusted to you. You take care of your body, mind and spirit. What you eat and drink affects the care you are giving to your body. What you eat and drink also reflects how you feel about yourself and your body. Think about all of the times in a day when you are making choices for yourself, and how each and everyone of those choices is a reflection of your self-love, your self-esteem.

Find a comfortable, quiet place where you can sit and reflect without being interrupted. Take a few moments to sit there, relax and reflect on these thoughts:

> Self-esteem is a reflection of self-love.
> Self-love arises out of self-acceptance.
> Self-acceptance comes from self-forgiveness.

Reflect on today and the choices you made today. What do they say about you?

Do the choices you made today reflect self-love, self-pride, self worth, self-esteem, and self-compassion? Do you begin to see how your choices affect your life?

Choose to grow from this moment.

HONOR

What a funny word. What does it mean? It's related to honesty. The word "honor" comes down to us, nearly intact as to spelling, from the ancient Romans. It has a wide variety of meanings. In the game of golf "having the honor" refers to having the privilege of playing first from the tee. In contract bridge, the "honor" cards are the cards with the highest value, the face cards and the ace in each suit.

But "honor" also shares a meaning with the words homage, deference and reverence. That shared meaning is "respect and esteem shown to another." Esteem, in turn, means "to set a high value on something," or "to regard highly and prize accordingly." So honor can be said to mean, "to treat with reverence and high regard, to value highly and prize worthily."

Let's take a moment to talk about self-esteem. If "esteem" means to set a high value on something or to regard something highly and to prize it reverently, then "self esteem" would mean that we value ourselves highly, that when we have high self esteem we treat ourselves with honor and reverence and respect. By regarding ourselves highly, I'm not referring to arrogance and conceitedness and power trips. I'm talking about being kind and nice to ourselves and treating ourselves with the same reverence and respect we would accord to our most precious treasure.

We each honor life itself by living our lives. Or perhaps some of us may dis-honor life itself by the way we live our lives. Each of us has been given the most amazing gift, the gift of life. It's the one thing we are given. The rest is up to us. We have to work for everything else. What we make of that precious gift of life and how we live our lives is up to each one of us. That's where self-esteem comes in. That's where each of us honoring ourself comes in.

EXERCISE FOUR

This exercise is about releasing, about letting go of part of that stick you use to beat yourself up with. Give yourself permission to release your past, and to sit with your honor.

Take a clean sheet of paper and find something to write with. Find a warm, sunny place and have a seat. It can be indoors or outdoors. If you feel like it, maybe take your shoes off. Just sit quietly and feel.

Breathe.

As soon as you can, start writing down what you feel about yourself right now. Be honest and write down whatever comes into your head. Good or bad. Take your time. Honor those feelings, good or bad.

Now sit with your writing. Fold it up and put it in a place that is special and private to you. Leave it there until you are ready to continue.

If what you wrote was negative, you have externalized a piece of your negative inner self by writing it down. When the time is right, throw your writing away, get rid of it, burn it, dispose of it. The physical act of this writing effort has harvested onto the paper some of the negative energy you have been keeping inside you and the writing down has transformed that energy into a physical object you can part with permanently.

If what you wrote was positive keep your writing. Put it somewhere special. Somewhere where you can find it and look at it later on. The good that we feel about ourselves is ours to keep and enjoy for the rest of our lives.

Now that we have the good feelings of trust, honor and self compassion, along with our writing and disposing mechanism to help us displace our negative feelings, let us proceed.

Looking back on our lives is something not all of us do. My father's mother is a good example of someone who did not look back on things that had happened in her life. When the subject of the past came up, she often would dismiss the subject by saying, "It's blood under the bridge." She made the phrase into a statement of resignation. She would say this particularly when an unpleasant subject from the past was mentioned. The feeling in her statement was cold and numbing and of being in slow motion, as if she was being swept away by some immovable force that she could not control. She rarely spoke of her childhood, and when she did it was usually some self-serving moment.

But you could tell she wasn't happy—her unhappiness showed on her face. Her facial expression seemed to say that she believed she was stuck with her past, but by God she was going to fight for all she could lay her hands on now. Her past was a closed book, but today and tomorrow were things she could handle. She was completely absorbed in my father's life, and that fact helped weaken several of his marriages. My grandmother shut herself off from her past, but there is an obverse, or counterpart, reaction to reviewing our pasts as well.

My father was a man who recounted his personal past as if it had happened that day. When I would ask him to tell me about his present day, he became rather dismissive about it, and gave only cursory details.

But his past? Now there's a story to be told. Today is just another day to get through. His involvement in people and events around him was limited, and usually those people and events only served as brief topics of conversation. He had buried any anger he felt about his past, and would not have a conversation about it under any circumstance. "Why bring that stuff up? It's over."

But it's not over. He's still angry. And it shows~ When he starts talking about his past, at first it is cast in a favorable light. Then that part of the story in his life ends, other memories crowd into his thought process and he falls silent.

Only alcohol changes this pattern. After he has had a few drinks, he becomes seized with the anger that he has buried all these years and he will lash out verbally at anything or any one near him. His lashing out lasts only a short while. And then he will fall silent. And his cycle will begin again.

Someone once said to him "I started life as a child." By this she was trying to convey to him that we all begin as untrained beings, or innocents, if you will, and that we have to work to become adult, that it's OK to talk about the past.

I remember his response. He said that her answer was "an excuse." He wasn't willing to give himself or anyone any slack. Today he remembers his childhood with sadness and regret.

I remember my childhood as well, but without regret. I have recaptured my personal past, and now I view its emerged landscape calmly, without rancor or remorse.

I have invested a goodly amount of work and a fair share of my time in order to get to the place where I can say that I can look at my personal past without regret. I understand the effort and commitment that this work takes and requires. I have spent, and continue to spend, a lot of time and effort working on resolving my past, but it did not become my raison d'etre or obsession.

Living in the "real time," in the here and now, was and is my raison d'etre. While I was working on my past earlier in my life, what I wanted to understand, both in my head and in my heart was, "Why was I the way I was? Did I have choice in my life?" Did I have any choice in the death of my mother? In the emotional brutality my grandmother inflicted upon me? In my father's use of alcohol? Where was choice?

WHY?

Why?
Why?

When I was growing up I used to ask, "Why?" I asked it a lot, especially of my parents. I know they loved me, and I have come to understand, both in my head and in my heart, that they also wanted the best for me. But their definition of what was best for me and the definition that I held of what was best for me were different, sometimes wildly so. I wanted to stay outside and play. They wanted me indoors. There would be a struggle. Eventually, my parents would win and/or I gave in. I know that last sentence sounds awkward, but linguistically it expresses my belief in how things work between people. No matter where you are in your life at this moment within any relationship you have, you are partially responsible. But only partially. No more and no less than 50.0%. Ever.

As a child my parents were two of my most influential teachers. I watched them like a hawk. Not just out of fear, which certainly was present, but also because these folks had POWER. They could go and do and say and be whatever they wanted. Or so it appeared to my child's eyes. And I watched and I learned, lots and lots of stuff. Some good, some bad. Quite a mixed bag, actually. Just like all people, my parents encompassed a marvelous range of expression. As they have aged, I have seen how they've "wound down" with time. And this has resulted in a narrowing of their range of expression.

If my parents won the arguments I had with them, at some point they won partly because I quit my end of the disagreement and gave in to them. Certainly my parents used what is now called "behavior modification." They used it in a wide variety of modes and methodologies, including corporal punishment. Even so, I do not think of myself as having been beaten, particularly. My mother was a slapper. She would slap me from time to time, when she felt she had been severely pushed and when she was under great strain. My father's techniques were much more varied. He combined fists and arms and hands and lungs in seemingly endless combinations. He was and is quite a vicious fighter. And a noisy one as well.

Today when I look back at those times with today's perspective, I can see more clearly how wonderfully instructive my parents were. They were "role models" in the most literal sense of those words. And, perhaps more importantly I can see quite clearly what a wonderful student I was, and how much I absorbed from my "role models."

Now my being a student of my parents' teachings may sound strange to you, but I came to discover that I was learning all the time. I am still learning today. I learned by conscious and unconscious means and for conscious and unconscious reasons. There are times when I have seen some part of one of my parents suddenly present in me. Sometimes this is funny, at other times it is quite a challenge.

As I have said, I used to jump right in and "beat myself up" for all the bad things I did to myself. I now see I was just doing to myself what my parents did to me, and now I know how destructive that was. Where my mother may have slapped me for being naughty I would beat myself up for a perceived naughtiness. Where my father might have pounded me with his fists and yelled at me for some real or imagined bad behavior I would indulge in some self-destructive behavior to punish myself for my misdoings.

As a result, I am having to learn how to re-parent myself, to take care of me, to love me. I am having to learn how to be a kind and loving and forgiving good parent to myself. It's not always easy to do this, but the rewards are priceless. And I am succeeding.

In the act of re-parenting myself I have worked at bringing to the surface any pain or hurt that I felt I received from Mom and

Dad over the years. For years I was told that I should forgive them for what they did, they "meant well." OK, fine, I can accept that. But then what do I do with my pain and anger? In a similar situation, what do you do with the pain and anger you have as a result of your parents' mistakes in parenting you? For many of us the answer has been that we stuff those feelings deep inside ourselves.

What I am saying is that these painful emotions which we feel, whether we express them or not, are real. They are not imaginings, fantasies or delusions. They are real. And for some reason, possibly even a long ago reason that we cannot now recall, we chose to stuff those hurting and painful feelings inside of ourselves. This process starts in our childhood.

Childhood is a singular time in our lives and is quite unique and special. Years ago in Los Angeles I remember meeting a man at a party who practiced "rebirthing." I was intrigued when he said that, if I wanted to, I could return to the moment of my birth, that the memories of that event were inside my head and that he could help me unlock them.

Some time later, long after that party, I came across his card and reflected on our conversation. As I began to seriously contemplate calling him I was suddenly confronted with a deep and painful burning in my lower chest. The intensity of the pain nearly doubled me over.

The burning and hurting continued while I struggled to the kitchen for some milk and then to the bathroom for some antacid or whatever before going to bed. I never did call that man, because when I woke up the next morning I knew there was something deep and ghastly inside me, some memory or memories that I was not ready to deal with at that time. I felt powerless in front of my fear. And as long as I felt that way I would be stuck. That is where change and choice enter the picture.

Years ago a man came to me for a consultation. He came because his then-girlfriend had suggested that he might get some "tips" on being more successful. All during our conversation, I kept feeling that this man had been ignored by his parents when he was very small, starting around his second birthday. When I asked him about it, he said, "No," he had no memories of his parents ever having been less than loving and kind to him. In fact he as quite positive that he had lived a wonderful childhood and became somewhat peeved with me for asking. Nevertheless we talked on and had a good discussion.

Weeks later he called me and we talked. He said that he had begun to have strange and troubling dreams about himself and his parents when he was a child. Finally in a spur of the moment he had asked his mother if she recalled his second birthday. She calmly replied that nothing out of the ordinary had happened. A few weeks later he spoke with his estranged elder sister who had called him needing his help on an unrelated matter. When he asked her if there was anything she could remember about any of his birthdays when he was little, she initially said "No," but as she talked on she suddenly remembered a terrible car crash that had happened sometime in the past and the bloody, mangled bodies that men had removed from one of the cars in the crash. Like a balloon, this incident expanded in his mind and he recalled his mother hysterically screaming, "Oh, my God" over and over.

Over the next few days, more and more memories flooded to his conscious mind. As he began to bring these troubling memories to the surface, he began to recall other events in his childhood. By examining and re-experiencing these "frozen memories," he began to become a calmer, more focused and loving man. He also understood why he had such a morbid fear and dread of squealing car tires squealing and the sounds of a car accident. He worked long and hard to examine and re-experience and understand those memories from his past. As a result of his work, today he is a happier man and much more at peace with his childhood.

Having a good life involves working at it. Change is work.

EXERCISE FIVE

The purpose of this exercise is to dispose of as much negative energy and negative emotion as you can, i.e., to get it out of your system.

Find some photographs of various periods during your childhood and make photocopies of the photos. Find a place where you feel safe and comfortable and where you will not be interrupted for a while. Have the photocopies and a writing implement with you. Relax. Get comfortable. Take a few deep breaths.

Now try to recall an incident from your childhood that affected you negatively, one that left you feeling hurt and pained. Take as much time as you need.

When you have an incident in mind and using the back (the blank side) of the photocopies you have made, write down everything you can recall about this incident. Try especially to write about all of the bad moments, the moments that caused you pain, whether physical or mental pain. If you can, try to write about the painful moments that still are painful to you when you recall them. Take as much time as you need and write as much as you like.

When you have finished, put your writing aside. Put it in a safe place where it will not be disturbed and where no one will find it.

When you are ready, and it may take a few minutes or a few days, transform your writing. Shred it, burn it, crumple it up, do anything you can to transform your writing. Then dispose of it. Get rid of it. Permanently. Repeat this exercise as often as you feel is necessary and beneficial to you.

You may feel drained and without energy after you complete this exercise. Do not be alarmed by the loss of energy you may feel—this is a normal reaction to completing an exercise like this. Rest and relax. You will feel better soon.

SUSAN

S usan always seemed to pick the wrong guys. Not that they were bad guys or anything, they just didn't work out. One day she started to see a pattern: she would love and give and care and share and make and do, but no matter what she did, it seemed to her that he didn't see it or feel it or know it or acknowledge it or use it. It drove her almost nuts.

Finally, she came to see me to work on it. As we talked about her series of lovers and guys she had been close to, one very salient and unmistakable fact emerged—she cared more about the man of the moment than she did about herself.

During our discussions, it also came out that Susan felt she had to be the stronger partner in her relationships. Although this did not always please her, she preferred it to being an equal or lesser part of the relationship. She wanted a caregiver, a man who was a giver, not a taker. And at some point, every man she met ran away from her. Finally she realized that this was a very old pattern. It had been going on for years and years. It all started with her father—the first of many men to run away from her. Same with her first husband. He ran away, too.

As Susan and I began to explore the reasons why her life was the way it was, she began to be aware of the changes she wanted to make so that her life would be richer and better and happier. She began to acknowledge her fears and to deal with the years of stored and pent-up emotions that her childhood had contained.

As our work continued, she saw how she had repeated her relationship with her father again and again. She replicated that relationship with almost every man she met when the relationship became an emotionally close one. And she began to see how in each successive relationship there came a point where she began to expect different reactions and words from the man and how she would become increasingly jealous, spiteful, sneaky, mean-spirited and supremely angry when those different words and responses didn't happen.

She choose to change. She did the work. She changed. Today she is happy.

SURVIVING ONE'S PARENTS

My father was an alcoholic. Aging decreased the amount of his drinking, but it did not lessen the severity of alcohol's effect on his old body. The cumulative effect of his years of drinking ruined his body, corrupted his thinking, stunted his feelings and left him a shell at the time of his death.

I used to believe that my dad was the way he was and that was it. This belief led me to sever all contact with him for 3 years. Then one day he telephoned me. I heard his voice and hung up the phone, flooded by waves of revulsion. I began to address the issue of why I was so repelled by the sound of my father's voice, even when it was just on the telephone. I worked very hard to understand my response to him. When he called again four years later, in the summer of 1987, I heard a different tone coming from him. This time, I heard a voice that sounded lonely, scared, in pain. This change on my part led to our re-opening our dialogue and relationship. It is important to note that I am taking responsibility for my actions here, as I am the one who heard a different tone of voice.

My father and I had a strange and strained relationship, probably since before the day I was born. The reason I say "probably" is that most folks who knew him then and who still remember those days don't want to recall what my father was like. For years I didn't want to think about or talk about or see my father. Even today, there are times when I still feel this way.

My parents met in a bar on York Boulevard in Highland Park, California in 1948. They married and started a funny kind of family. Funny because my father had custody of his daughter from his first marriage and my mother had custody of her son from her first marriage. The two children were close in age but nothing else. My parents fought about money and sex and parents and the past.

Leaving their children with my father's mother they drove to Mammoth Lake, California to enjoy the 4th of July, 1950. They stayed in their friend Dean's cabin. They made me. I was born in 1951.

My parents divorced in 1952. My mom went to her mother's with me and my half-brother. My father went on the prowl for another woman.

My mom met and married a very human man. She died in 1965 and I went to live with my father. From the minute my dad took me to my his house and left me there alone, I knew my life would never be the same.

Today I understand that my father failed to become distinct or different in character from his mother, my grandmother. In other words, he failed to differentiate from her. This lack of differentiation from his mother led to my father being labeled weak and a Momma's boy by his ex-girlfriends and wives.

In his house there was room for one male only—him. I was another, and threatening, male living in the same household. So I was subjected to words and actions by and from my father that caused me to seek therapy for a long time in order to recover and heal from those words and actions.

And what did all the therapy and healing say to me? It told me to look back on my relationships with my parents. It taught me to allow myself to feel what I felt, to not suppress my emotions.

For years I feared ever becoming a parent, or even caring for children. My dealings with children made me uncomfortable, although I could not say why. As a teenager, I felt antsy around children and avoided them as often as possible. I remember one day when a woman told me that I would make a good parent. I laughed on the outside, but inwardly I cringed at the thought. Me, a father? Never!

My reaction was so immediate and so strong that my friend looked at me with an unasked question on her face. Suddenly I

knew that there was some deeper and darker feeling lingering inside
of me. Anger, shame, fear, panic—I was frozen by my emotions.
Memories of my childhood's hardest and most tragic moments
flooded my mind. I turned away from her, unable to watch her
reaction that I so clearly anticipated and feared. She kindly stopped
talking and left me with my feelings.

Later that night, alone, at home in bed, I thought about why
I had such a strong and nearly overpowering feeling about becoming
a father. As I let my thoughts wander, I began to imagine the fun
I would have with a little person who was looking at the world
through new eyes. As I continued to imagine that child, quite
suddenly and unexpectedly I found myself crying. I was
dumbfounded by the wetness on my face and touched my cheek
in amazement.

Suddenly my Dad burst through my bedroom door with an
angry and drunken look on his face. He snarled at me. Then he
spat out the words. "Tears like a baby," and slammed the door
shut. Later, he crept down the hall to my door and cracked open
the door. I pretended to be asleep. I guess my Dad went away, but
I didn't hear him.

I lay there in the dark and felt safe. Moments passed and the
door didn't move. I took a deep breath and sighed. And cried. The
tears stung my cheeks as a pain from somewhere deep near my
soul seared through my right side twisting up to exit through my
right shoulder.

Years later, I encountered the concept that we choose our
parents. I remember laughing when I heard that teaching. For
some of us, these people we call parents are the most important
people we ever deal with in life. For me, the majority of my
personal "work" has been around healing the relationships I
have with my parents.

My work has made it possible for me to differentiate between
the idealized image I have of a perfect (for me) Father and Mother
and the realities, the real people that I have chosen. And yes, I do
believe I chose them, but I have no desire to see myself as a victim

of some god or of some system that would subject me a particular fate. I see my parents as the teachers who started me on the path of my life.

What I have made of that life is because of them and because of me.

More me than them, however.

MELISSA

Melissa hated her father. She had never met him but he had given her and her mother up and Melissa hated him. She didn't speak to him for years and years. Then one day a letter came in the mail, addressed in a handwriting she didn't recognize. Her hands trembled as she read the words her mother wrote. Her mother had re-met Melissa's father and had been out to dinner and a movie with him in the week just passed.

She put down the letter, stunned by what she had read. Her mother was with the enemy. Melissa felt strangely betrayed and confused. Why her father? Why now?

She picked up the letter and read on. Her mother wrote that her father had explained that he had left their marriage rather than face his own failure. Now he wanted to make amends. He wanted to see where he stood. As they had talked, Melissa's mother had felt that lump in her throat when she looked at him that night, under streetlights. She found that she was still in love with him. She was thinking about becoming serious in the relationship.

Melissa was devastated.

Several times she refused to meet him. Each time her mother mentioned him, Melissa would interrupt and change the subject. This went on for 27 months, until one day Melissa's mother called and said she and her father were reaffirming their marriage vows, as they had never divorced.

Melissa stood in her kitchen and felt hot tears fill her eyes, felt light-headed and woozy, her mouth dry and throat tight. She hung up the phone. She took more than 300 aspirins. She nearly died.

When she awoke in the hospital, he was standing there looking at her with tears in his eyes. She knew immediately who he was. He sobbed thanks to God and cried and sobbed. Something in

Melissa vanished. She looked at this man and felt love and compassion and peace. Whatever pain and hurt and anger she had repressed was gone. From that time they came to know each other, as parent-child, as adults, as friends. They have done some therapy together, which has helped them over the rough spots and shown them the resources on which they can each draw to have a balanced and healthy relationship.

Today if you ask her who helped her recover her wellness she will tell you, "My father."

EXERCISE SIX

The purpose of this exercise is to dispose of pain associated with bad memories from your past.

Find some photographs of your family taken during various periods during your childhood and make photocopies of the photos.

Find a place where you feel safe and comfortable and where you will not be interrupted for a while. Have the photocopies and a writing implement with you. Relax. Get comfortable. Take a few deep breaths.

Now try to recall some bad times from your childhood associated with the people in the photographs, times that left you feeling hurt and pained. Take as much time as you need.

When you are ready, and using the backs of the photocopies you have made, start writing about the bad times you remember. Try not to edit your thoughts or feelings. Just let the words flow. Take as long as you wish.

When you have finished, put your writing aside. Put it in a safe place where it will not be disturbed and where no one will find it.

When you are ready, and it may take a few minutes or a few days, transform and dispose of your writing. Shred it, burn it, crumple it up, do anything you can to transform your writing. Then dispose of it. Get rid of it. Permanently.

Repeat this exercise as often as you feel is necessary and beneficial to you.

What we are working on here is getting rid of the painful parts of our past. Doing this will involve effort and resolve. And time. It won't happen at the snap of one's fingers. Resolve to be as you want to be, and not the victim of undissipated energy from your childhood.

FAMILY

Some of our most enduring and difficult relationships are in our families. When I was a teenager, I would visit my friends' homes and sometimes meet their parents or whoever lived with them. I knew one kid whose mom who was a pot and speed addict. She was always acting either stoned and not-quite-with-it or talking and gesturing so quickly that she would sometimes blur before my eyes. This kid's dad ran a record company and he was always sneaking around with much younger women with big chests. The kid was a needy and mean liar.

Although I do not know where these people are today, I wish them well. I learned from them.

Sometimes the sights that appear before our eyes are negative and destructive. Sometimes the people and situations we see are ugly and mean and harmful.

And those negative and destructive and ugly and mean and harmful things can affect us. We can internalize the pain or anger or trauma and we poison ourselves from within with that pain or anger or trauma. Then life begins to resemble a one-two punch: the scenes we see, and the attendant emotions are one punch. The reactive emotion to what we have seen is the second punch, for now we carry around inside us the negative emotions brought on by what we have seen.

We see these terrible things and we take them in. That is to say that we are affected emotionally by viewing this information. People sometimes react before they are over-stimulated.

I know of a man who seems quite nice and friendly, but since his son's birth he has had a hairtrigger response to his son's actions when those actions have not measured up to what he, as a father, wanted to see in his son. Today both father and son admit to sharing a "chilly" relationship, and neither wishes to work at changing it. The son is perceived as a timid and very shy young man. What people don't know or see is how he used to take out his stored aggressions on small animals. That was how our paths crossed.

He joined a men's group I was in. Eventually, he came to a point where he could tell us of his actions with the animals and his profound anguish as a result. He worked with a caring and wise woman who helped him to understand what had happened in his life and why he had done what he had done. Today he channels his angers into positive and constructive paths: he is regarded as one of the better veterinarians in his area.

Anger is a very difficult emotion for most of us.

EXERCISE SEVEN

Find a comfortable place with a table and chair where you won't be interrupted. Close the door if that will help. Find a pen and paper.

Sit down, relax and take several deep breaths. Perhaps take off your shoes.

When you are relaxed and comfortable, take up the pen and write a letter to each of your parents. The letter should express to each parent exactly how you feel about him or her. Do not hold back, do not try to put a positive spin on your feelings. Write whatever you feel is important to write.

When you have finished, re-read your letter.

Tale a few moments to reflect. Try to put yourself in the shoes of the parent to whom you wrote. Then ask yourself if receiving this letter will make the relationship between you and that parent a better one. Give this question your honest and careful consideration.

If you decide that the letter will improve your relationship with the parent to whom you wrote it, send the letter.

If you do not think the letter will improve your relationship with the parent to whom you wrote, dispose of the letter in an appropriate manner. Burn it, shred it, crumple it up. Get rid of it.

Repeat as needed.

ON DESPAIR

Linda sat at the typewriter trying to focus on the page in the carriage before her. The typewriter sat where a sewing machine had been before, a gift that was never explored. Her eyes stung and there was a dull, insistent throb in the back of her head. Her mouth was dry, she felt dry. She was at a point of just exploding inside, her mind racing along never seizing on one thought or impulse, and yet she sat motionless at her table, paralyzed by the deep and chaotic emotions inside her.

Ever had that feeling? Just numb with the emotional turmoil and physically stuck in one spot? That is the feeling of despair. Despair is a clinging weight, and a gnawing apprehension that lurks just below the surface. It can be very hard to throw off, but it can be done.

Being immobilized by our emotions is sometimes a frequent and scary thing. The shame and embarrassment of it occasionally preclude us from talking about it, even to close friends.

The mistake we often make is to see our emotions as "the enemy". Then we try to distance ourselves as far as we can from those feelings and those thoughts. We will go to terrible lengths to try to avoid ourselves and our feelings, all because of fear. Fear is the active side of despair.

Despair. An old word in the world's languages. When you read old stories, whether sacred or secular, you will come across this word. It means to lose all confidence. It is a core emotion, to be sure, but like all things in nature it has a balancer.

That balancer is hope.

Don't fight it. Feel it . . . let it sink in . . . go with it. Feel hopeful. Say "I hope" out loud. It is the only word that can vanquish despair. Say it again.

Take a deep breath. Breathe in thinking the word hope, Say it again. HOPE.

I remember a time in my life when I sat, stoned on marijuana. I felt light and happy, a mild sense of euphoria, my discerning adult voice now says. I had gone over to my friend Mike Gold's house, and his younger sister, Ellen, had gotten some "weed" from somewhere. We went out behind the dumpster and smoked this little pinwheel of a thing. I felt wonderful.

I remember being happy that afternoon there in Van Nuys. It was a warm summer day, I wasn't in summer school, and I was spending the night at Mike's. His mother, Harriet, told me she would forever be my Jewish mother. Harriet was strong and gentle, opinionated and reflective, truly a wonderful woman. That night was probably nothing special to Mike or his family, but to me it was a reminder that I had been happy once, that I had been loved and wanted and accepted and believed. As we sat sharing dinner, I saw love and acceptance in those eyes around that table.

The next morning, when I returned to my father's house, I was met by eyes that spoke to me of leaving and never returning, of disappearing if I chose. Anything, but I should just leave. I was 14 years old.

I remember the pain in my chest as I crossed that threshold, moving past my grandmother, hoping I wouldn't brush against her, hoping she wouldn't strike out at me, or say something ugly as I entered my father's house.

Such despair.

I felt trapped and alone and confused and afraid. I could not imagine my life getting better. Despair is like an emotional black hole, it sucks you in and paralyzes you. You become drab and dull, drained of so much good and hope and joy and peace.

Stuck.

Hopeless.

Sometimes we stay here awhile, sometimes we change.

Sometimes we get into blame. In our anger and frustration we lash out at others, sometimes at complete strangers. Our emotions boil over into focusing on others and ignoring ourselves. If we stay in this channel, we sometimes become victims. Then we feel justified in our blaming, and become more passive-aggressive, striking out and then acting wounded when someone strikes back. Most of us know people like this. Sometimes we are people like this.

To resolve this problem of coping without despair we must know what is at the root of it, what is the basic thought or feeling or belief underpinning this negative manifestation from within us?

So give yourself over to whatever pain or anger or shame or whatever is at the bottom of this response/reaction. Stop trying to suppress it and let yourself feel it. Let it wash over you. Experience it now and let it leave you. Think of all of the useful energy that you use to suppress and store these dreadful feelings. Imagine using that energy for a good and worthwhile purpose. It can be done. The choice is yours.

A long time ago I worked with a woman who, in a brief flash, revealed that she would sometimes sit in a chair in her living room for hours at a time. At first she did it when her husband and children were gone from the house. Gradually she began to do it when the kids came home.

Being caught up in living their own lives, they didn't notice their mother's behavior. The first time her husband observed her, he took her action to indicate stress and fatigue and promptly arranged a vacation for them both. But as time passed it became evident to him that something was wrong. He called around and tried several different forms of approach and methodology, time after time. In time, he came to me. What he wanted was his wife back, by whatever means necessary. Living like this was pulling each of them apart.

At our first meeting, I asked her to set a timer when she sat in her favorite chair in the living room. It took a couple of times for her to remember to do this, but the first time she did set the timer, she set it for 20 minutes. She never heard it ring, and "returned" three hours later when her husband came home from work.

When she was asked what she felt during these periods, she would reply, "Fine," but this was also her standard response to any question about how she felt.

In time she did the one thing that saved her and her family. She gave in to her feelings. She stopped fighting inside. She became very depressed. Her depression lasted for several weeks. She lost weight. She had to take time off from her job. She had to take care of herself

For years she had been told that her life was so wonderful. Her beautiful and loving parents showered her with gifts galore. She heard countless times that she "had everything one could ever want."

Deep down inside, though, she felt ugly and angry and stupid and mean. But she had to keep these feelings under lock and key, buried deep inside her, because they didn't fit in with "having everything one could ever want" that she had been told so often.

Now she was at a time when she could no longer shove her dark feelings and thoughts away, and the struggle to keep control of herself and her feelings was immobilizing her.

Our work together revolved around her expressing her feelings, of giving voice to her darker side. She began to acknowledge her pain and hurt. She was able to cry for the first time since she was four years old. In her struggle to free herself from a self-imposed prison, she began to make changes in her self and in her life. Today she is a very happy soul.

EXERCISE EIGHT

This exercise is to help you learn to trust yourself more fully.

Find a comfortable, safe place where you won't be interrupted. Close the door if you like. Sit down. Loosen or take off your shoes.

So. What to do with your deep and dark feelings? Breathe. Don't fight it. "Fighting it" is what has kept whatever is buried with your psyche trapped and locked and unchanging.

Go with your feelings, even though it may be difficult and scary at first. Let those feelings come up.

The universe is not out to get you.

Relax. Breathe. Release your fear.

Breathe.

What did you feel? What "popped" into your head, into your heart? Take a look at it, whatever it is. This is something that is now up and before you and it is time to work on resolving it, so you can get on with living a fulfilling and enjoyable life.

Keep breathing and do some work.

Try writing down your thoughts, or if you choose, share them with someone you trust. But get them out of you. Make them separate from you in reality. Write them down or say them out loud.

Life is not a dress rehearsal. Love yourself enough to get to the bottom of your being. We all have "stuff" to deal with. After all, we are merely human beings. And that is saying a whole bunch. We are really something quite special.

We are alive.

ON BELIEF

What a marked contrast there is between today and my earlier years. Today I am happy, loved and in love, well and cared for, by myself and others. I don't live each day on the edge, or anywhere near it.

Magic? Drugs? Denial? None of the above. And yet all played a part. In my years on the face of this planet the most amazing things have happened in my life—the issues that have confronted me, and my handling of them. Each and every day has been another day of learning opportunities for me. There hasn't been a single day when something did not occur that was not news to me.

I have come to see that certainly in my life, and perhaps in others as well, the right thing always happens, and that life (or God or what or whoever) has never given me more than I can handle. To be sure there have been times when I have been sorely and surely tested: each and every moment involves another opportunity to choose. There have been some very hard choices. And along the way there has been pain and hurt and confusion and a whole universe of emotions and feelings and thoughts.

And always the opportunity for growth.

No, it hasn't always been just the way I want it to be. But then the universe and life do not revolve around me. There are 6 billion other people with whom I share this little orb.

When I let my ego get out of control it spins me around, and makes me more than dizzy. We see them every day, those folks being held hostage by their egos. In fact, sometimes we are "hijacked" by our egos, and taken "away." And countless folks have confused self-esteem and ego. It's easy to do. I know.

EXERCISE NINE

This exercise is to help you come to a deeper understanding of who you are.

1. Upon arising, as you pass the first mirror you notice, stop long enough to look into your own eyes and say, not think, "I love you,"
2. Each time you see a mirror or a reflection of yourself, say "I love you" to yourself.

On the morning of the fourth day observe how you feel when you see a mirror. Do you feel lighter, better? If not, repeat some of the prior exercises to see if there is some blockage to your feeling better.

LORNA

She loved him, and she knew he wouldn't mess up her birthday. Today she was 21. Legal in every state, a full adult member of society with all its rights and privileges, so help her God.

Last night had been a drifty one, what with him rolling allover as usual, grabbing at her from time to time in a sleepy, dreamy way. She was hoping that the coming morning would find them nestled like old lived and loved spoons, softly cradled and held gently, firmly to the bosom of love.

21 wasn't easy for her.

When her path crossed mine in this life, she was on general assistance and food stamps—ruing her "no good white trash whore of a mother from hell" and cursing her perceived fate.

And that is really the message here: there is no such thing as fate. You are an agent of free will and are free to be as you choose. It is up to you. Period.

I've told not a few people that if fate exists, then we are not free. Our lives are then controlled by someone or something else. I don't like the sound of that, not even the idea. It strikes me as a convenient and easy way out, off the hook. I have a part to play in my life, a part that will help determine how my life turns out. To take away one's part in life is to become a passive creature, at the will of others. Sounds too akin to "victim" to me.

Lorna believed that she was how she was because of her mother, and she blamed all of the poor choices she made as her mother's fault, and if her mother had not done something or said something Lorna's life would have been a damned sight better. Lorna and I have had conversations for many years now. She is a mother twice over, with a beautiful boy and a new and precious girl. She and her mother battled to have the last say as to who was right for a while longer, but Lorna began to remember the good and kind memories too, and her heart softened.

Today they are friends and good traveling companions who annually jet off to China or Turkey or points divers for the joy of it. Lorna's mistake with Keith, her boyfriend mentioned above, was that her feelings about care-taking were her own unexpressed needs and seen by Lorna as Keith's needs. This is known as projection.

We learn to undervalue ourselves for a variety of reasons, none of them good. With each successive exposure to negative self-assessment, our self-esteem is eroded and can eventually die, along with the rest of us.

Lorna had been beaten down by an abusive and emotionally absent father and a weak and scared mother. Her father was mad at his own mother and could not and would not express those feelings out of fear of his older and richer brother for whom he worked. Her father's anger was directed at his wife and his daughter, Lorna and her mother. He had been raised by a mother who rebuked him in public as being "slow but kind". Although Lorna's mother hated her own mother with a blind fury, she directed it into her religion, where she cried about all the suffering in the world to those who would listen.

Lorna grew up believing she was weak and spacey and just a little weird.

Getting breasts had nearly killed her of embarrassment as her mother had insisted on Lorna baring her chest to her mother when asked, which was usually twice a year until Lorna was 16, at which time her mother's control issues shifted south, so to speak, and virginity reared its confused but lofty head.

Lorna lost her virginity to a nervous but gentle man when she was 28. Keith, who had been first her secret crush at 17, had become her serious boyfriend by Lorna's 21st birthday. She did not have the chance to offer up her precious gift that night because Keith got picked up at the market by a man in his thirties who had taken him home and eventually had given Keith money for his time. Lorna saw him 4 days after her birthday and they fought and he dumped her for an older woman with money.

She finally left him one day, a day when the clouds in the sky were steel grey, peering at them through the stiff and brittle sheer curtains in their bedroom. She relinquished her hopes with him and chose to get on with her life. Whatever she had believed about hell stopped flickering in her mind. It was time to get out.

Packing the kids' stuff had been hard, especially because her rib hadn't completely healed from the last time, but she got it done. The woman's shelter had been just perfect. The folks there had been so calm and welcoming, she felt safe. Keith wouldn't hurt her here.

Lorna was in line at the Catholic Worker kitchen near skid row in Los Angeles. We talked some. Amazing woman, a giant in heart and deed. She chose. She risked. She did something about it. She did not "make it happen."

She opened up a part of her emotional armor and permitted a differing thought to linger. Specifically, that she was ready to stop running and crawling and later, hating herself.

Three years later, on the dole, she met me at a volunteer center where she was making a little money. We began just shooting the breeze, and got down to brass tacks about four weeks later and did some serious work for five years. It remains a joy to remember Lorna's emergence from her fear and anger and pain.

The right thing happens, especially if you encourage it.

DISPLACEMENT

Energy is manifested in us physically and emotionally. Some of our emotions are associated with negative energy and some with positive energy. When we express our emotions and feelings, we are exhibiting energy. And when we push our emotions and feelings down inside us, we are suppressing the energies associated with those emotions and feelings.

So here is my understanding of what happens to the anger we feel but do not express. It becomes trapped in our bodies and forms pools in many places in our bodies. This, in turn, leads to disease and/or fat and eventually kills us. Think about it. What happens to all the negative energy we feel when we're angry?

A man I once knew told me that when he got angry he would ball up his fist five times and then it was over. He was right.

A woman I knew would write down the "evil doer's'" name and then tear up the paper and that was that. She was positively correct.

Most of us, when angered, dwell on it. We think about it again and again. All we are really doing is burning that negative energy into our living cells. And the body replicates itself time and time again. The living cells are constantly replacing themselves. So the negative energy stays with us, and keeps growing and growing. And so on and so on. It becomes an endless cycle and eventually kills us.

Sometimes our anger gets expressed and externalized. This is good.

Sometimes it does not get expressed and externalized. This is not good.

This is the start of disease.

Terrible things have happened to me during my lifetime. I have worked very hard at not repressing my feelings but instead worked to find ways to help me release the tension in my body. I found ways to express and externalize my anger because I did not want to be the victim of that anger, and I recognized that repressing it would make me that victim. Sometimes I could feel the rage begin to boil within me—the anger that seemed to blot out my logical mind and leave me prey to my emotions.

Societal conditioning taught me either to "stuff" my anger deep inside or to take it out in sports and other competitions. This spilled into nearly every facet of my life so that I was in a race with everyone whom I thought was better than I. The lower my self-esteem sank, the lower my race companion's self esteem sank, and yet I would continue to compete on some ego level. It was pathetic.

It became a downward spiral. I hit rock bottom in a car crash. What a wake up call extraordinaire that car crash was.

Storing anger in our bodies takes one of two forms: fat or disease. The energy of our anger must be dispersed or it will stay with us either as fat or as incipient disease. Medicine, for all of its advances, has yet to show us the formative device behind disease and illness.

Look around you. What is the source of fat, if not energy? Yes, people can change their diet, but until they change their behavior, they don't have an easy time of it and the endless cycle of diet, re-gain, diet, re-gain continues.

Consider this: the key to your wellness lies within you. All you need to do is to consider it as a possibility. Just give the idea a little bit of room in your thoughts. Call it a flight of fantasy, if you wish, but allow the concept to sit with you, so to speak.

So, on to displacement. The next page will ask you to consider this proposition more deeply.

EXERCISE TEN

This exercise will help you to more fully integrate a new personal view of yourself, starting with your physical body. Find a writing implement and some blank paper. Find a comfortable place where you will not be disturbed. Sit down and relax. If you wish, remove your shoes. Breathe and relax. Write down the negative things you feel about your body. Be honest.

Now tear up the piece of paper and throw it away.

This process can be repeated as often as you like to help you begin to change your view of you on a physical level. This displacement takes the energy you felt in your anger and releases it through transmutation.

It's that simple.

Practice of it can amaze you.

Consistency of practice can heal you.

ON *ANGER*

There have been times in my life when I seriously considered suicide. Perhaps considering is not precise enough. I reached the point where I was analyzing various methods to self-kill, ranking which would be more painful, how long each would take, which stood a better chance of really killing me, not just maiming me. I did not want to wake up later and find myself still alive.

To this day I remember a time, walking back to my father's house, and day-dreaming about the life I would have someday. When I really thought about how that could possibly happen, I got a whopping headache that silenced all subsequent thoughts. The futility of my situation would just as suddenly grab me and plunge me back into an abyss, a place of emotional and sometimes physical paralysis.

My life had become so bad, so desperate and bleak, that I could not see a way out of the pain and turmoil and anguish and anxiety that it had become. Death, that scary boogie-man, that hobgoblin that strikes terror in most people's hearts, suddenly wasn't so scary for me. In fact, death began to look somewhat attractive, especially when I considered the life that lay around and before me. I frankly didn't see any other way out of my situation. For much of that time, I believed it was hopeless. But I'd get back at them, I'd show them. I'd kill myself and make them feel bad, just like I did.

I prayed that my life would change. And to escape the pain I took a lot of drugs a lot of the time. Denial . . . ? No. Not denial. Symptomatic behavior. Learned behavior.

At the time described above, he was 51 and I was 16. I had never dreamed that I would strike him, or that he would strike me. He had never been particularly physical with me, except for the occasional and extremely rare spanking.

So the huge and nearly overwhelming explosion of anger and fury within me came as a terrible surprise when my father struck me the first time. I now remember standing in the den of his house and hearing his mother shout some word that broke the moment, stayed his hand and kept him from striking me again. It has taken me the better part of the past 20 + years to learn to deal with that anger.

I was unable to sustain fighting with my dad on a daily basis, and I felt quite powerless in many parts of my life. So I released my anger by finding somebody I could beat up on. And when I could express my anger, I was seethingly angry. "Very bad tempered" doesn't even begin to approach and wrath and rage I had within me.

I did find someone to beat up on. Me.

Drugs, denial, lies, accusation, the list goes on and on. My life was a living hell. My anger found a great target in me, because I could dredge up any mistake or blunder I made and just use this "evidence" as justification for my deplorable behavior. And of course guilt jumped right in there, too. There was no way out of this slime pit, with every action being yet another potential screw-up. "Give up, don't struggle," I told myself. "Just get stoned." Sleep. Anything, as long as I didn't have to deal with my stuff. I didn't have much of a life. It was little wonder that "self deliverance" looked so good. Or at times it seemed to.

But instead I turned my anger against myself in less immediately destructive ways and used "substances" to punish myself. My father's self-punishment weapon of choice was alcohol. For years, I believed that this thing—booze—was to blame for his unhappiness. Now I know that the booze was just a symptom, the outside, and that my father's emotions were the real problem, that they were what was tearing him up inside.

Writing the above words propelled me through time back to the grim reality of those memories. How horrible that time was, how scared and lonely and desperate I was. What a marked contrast to my life now.

I am happy, loved and in love, well and cared for, by myself and others. I don't live each day on the edge, or anywhere near it.

Anger is part of being human, and it is O.K. to get angry. As children we learn this, but with a twist. We hear words from our parents such as "stop that before I punish/scold/spank you." Right there we witness anger in our parent, but if we display our own anger, most likely our display of our anger will result in an emotional escalation on our parent's part. And the parent gets angrier. Bad move.

So we repress our anger and hope it goes away . . . but it doesn't.

"Dear God,

Please make Mommy stop hitting me. It hurts. I know she and Daddy yell, and I hide 'cause I'm scared. But Mommy will hit me when she finds me. Please make Mommy and Daddy stop yelling."

I found this letter in a child's reading book a few years ago when I worked with school age children. These particular parents always appeared to be calm, loving, supportive parents. The little boy who wrote this note had begun to become aggressive during play with others. After finding the note, I started talking with the child about his feelings, especially about his anger. He told me about his mother hitting him, beating him actually. Shortly after that, his mother came into the school instead of just dropping him off, and I took the chance of talking with her.

As we talked, she began to ask about her son. Then she blurted out that she was beating him and she dissolved in tears. We both cried. I suggested she seek counseling, which she agreed might help things. And she did start working on her life. The beatings stopped immediately. Her son began to work out his problems as well, and he became much more trustful and loving.

Today that child as grown into a well-balanced young man, and is now a very good father to his own children. He has purged himself of the terrible anger that his childhood engendered. He has successfully worked to resolve outstanding issues and not be plagued by them as so many of us are.

One of today's social mores is the belief that anger is bad and must be avoided at all times and at all costs. Once, at a party, I heard two people talking about an absent third named Bob. "Too bad he's such an angry guy," said the woman. The man agreed and told how he had heard that Bob had been passed up for a promotion at work and was quite bitter about it.

Later that evening I met Bob. He was rather dour and sullen. And all I could sense when I was around him was that no one had ever told Bob that internalized and repressed anger doesn't stay hidden forever, and that his anger was valid.

Not good, not bad, not understandable, not shameful, not a sign of a greater psychological breakdown, just valid. Just anger. Bob and I worked together for a while. Together we found a way to help him lose his anger and replace it with peace. The key was for him to begin to see that his parents are just his parents. They are just two people, not all people. Now that he has done the work around differentiation between his parents as archetypes and as people in general, he is the CEO of a thriving five-year-old Silicon Valley corporation. Healthy and happy.

Anger—such a human response. Do you remember the last time you became angry? What did you do with the energy of that anger? Did you yell or hit something or hold it in? Years ago, a friend and I went to see the film "Network." I was so thrilled when actor Peter Finch's character told his audience to go to the window and shout, "I'm mad as hell and I'm not gonna take it any more."

On the drive back home, we both stuck out heads out of the car windows and followed the character's instructions. We shouted. It felt so liberating and freeing and good.

I have come to recognize that energy is matter. If I become angry about something or someone I have choices to make: do I get rid of this energy or do I hold it in and slowly poison my system with it?

For me, the solution has been to let the anger out, to actively get rid of it. Sometimes I write letters, sometimes I shout at the walls, sometimes I throw stones into the ocean . . . The point is that I do something physical. I use energy to expel energy. I do not want the anger to make a home inside me, to live there and shorten my life. So I use that anger energy to do some physical act. That physical act is a vehicle for me to express my feelings, to release whatever feelings (anger or whatever) are inside me.

Say that, "What is done is done, and that there is nothing that we can do with the feelings left inside us, and in time they will go away or somewhere."

And that is true.

And that somewhere where they go is inside us, in our bodies, in our selves.

I remember a friend's mother from the time when I was in high school. She was always smiling when she thought people were looking. But I saw her once with a look of terror frozen on her face, her mouth a soft pink circle of mute witness to some unseen horror. Later, I saw the same face again, when I came out of a bathroom in her house and surprised her. She almost immediately composed her face into its smile, but I had seen her other side, her dark side.

The problem is one of being human, of yin and yang, bad and good, sweet and sour, light and dark. This duality is a natural expression of the duality that exists throughout the cosmos as we know it.

EXERCISE ELEVEN

This exercise will help you displace some of that old anger that is lodged within you.

Find a comfortable place where you can relax and where you won't be interrupted. Bring some blank sheets of paper and a writing implement.

Sit down and relax.

Breathe.

Take some time to sit and think about someone with whom you're angry.

Take the first person who jumps into your mind. Just one person.

Think/feel what it is you're angry about, about what it is that makes you angry.

Write down what it you're angry about and what it is about that person that angers you. Stop writing when you run out of anger.

Read your writing aloud.

Destroy it. Tear it up, burn it, anything to destroy it.

R epressing anger takes a lot of energy.
          I know of a woman who seldom left her bed because
she was so physically weak. She told me stories about growing up
with a sullen mother and a raging father. She told me how she had
married a man to escape her parents, and how her husband had
slowly become abusive toward her, both sexually and verbally. She
spent the time with her husband in fear, constantly aware of his
slightest indication of displeasure. Catering to his every whim left
her drained and in tears. She could barely make it to her bed after
he left the house in the morning, and she would sleep until she
heard him return.

After years of this life, she sought help and we worked together
to help her get rid of her repressed anger. At first, she denied that
she was any angrier than normal. Actually, she thought she got the
shorter end of the stick but she said she didn't mind. I asked her to
keep a daily record of her high and low moods.

A pattern of poor days began to emerge and as it did, she
began to recognize her anger and to acknowledge it. She began to
release her anger in ways that were safe. She started by writing
down her feelings, and then burning what she had written, to
expand further on the motif of releasing her negative energy. As
she began to write out her feelings, she became aware of painful
and hurtful memories that she had suppressed and of her anger
surrounding those memories. She transferred that anger into the
physical act of destroying something else, of venting her anger.

She started sleeping less, but more soundly. She began to eat
less, but her physical energy increased. Life brightened. She took
some classes at a junior college. Later, she got a job. Despite all of

her attempts to help her husband, her marriage deteriorated and came to an end.

Today she is divorced and very happy. Friends tell her that she looks years younger. She, herself, says that for the first time, she feels that she truly looks forward to tomorrow.

Her life is good.

Feelings are composed of energy in that they are electrical impulses in the brain. This energy, if not dispersed, will settle in the body. The energy needs body mass to stay, so some of us get fat and others burn out parts of our bodies.

Rather simple idea, but elusive at times, to be sure.

So take a moment now and reflect on the anger you felt today. What was it about?

If you can recall something you are storing anger. You might release it. Then again you may choose not to. It is your life. You are free to choose.

I ask you to consider choosing to forgive yourself. I ask you to look at yourself in a mirror and say into your own eyes, "I love you" until you can keep your gaze into your eyes and feel peaceful and complete.

Give yourself permission to change and grow.

EXERCISE TWELVE

This exercise will relieve some of the stress that repressed anger causes.

Find a place that's comfortable for you and where you won't be disturbed. Bring with you some blank sheets of paper and a writing implement. Sit down. Relax. If you wish, remove your shoes.

Take several deep breaths.

Think of all those people with whom you are angry. Make a list of them.

Now, next to each name, jot down why you're angry with that person.

Write a letter to the first person you listed. Tell him or her what you are angry about and why. Do not hold back your emotions. Do not rationalize your response. If necessary and/or desired, look at a photograph of this person while you are writing your letter.

When you are ready, go outside and read your letter out loud. When finished, ask yourself, "Mail it or burn it?"

Follow your decision.

SOMATIC REPRESSION

We do some interesting things in our modern society. One of them is to stigmatize alcohol and drug use. We regard as diseases certain behaviors connected with alcohol and drug use and treat those "diseases" as if they were problems. But they are not true problems. They are merely symptoms of emotional pain.

Stigmatizing them just adds another log to the fire and only makes matters worse.

What comes next?

For a while I worked down around skid row in L.A. One of the most interesting men I ever met was there, having soup at the Catholic Worker Kitchen one day. He was sick with a chest cold. I didn't have the heart to ask him to leave so I talked with him and tacitly gave him permission to remain behind after he had finished his soup. He had been a scientist at Los Alamos. He had met Oppenheimer and other nuclear scientists and knew a thing or two about recent history.

The pressure in this man's life mounted with his marriage and then after the birth of his disabled child. He began to drink. His wife began to drink. His wife and child were killed one day by a supposedly drunken driver who swerved into his wife's car, sending her down an embankment and into a wall where her car exploded. He doesn't remember much after that for a while.

When I met him, he had been on Skid Row for a few years, doing odd jobs now and then, when it rained or got too cold, and then using his earnings to sleep in some flop house for a while.

He was beginning to want more out of life. He said he wanted to be more secure in his later years, and not like some of the other guys he saw every day. He'd stopped drinking for the most part, and didn't get drunk any more. He said the feeling of starting to get drunk scared him and shut him down emotionally. He would stop drinking immediately and drink several glasses of water until it was time to sleep.

He had been through a "stop drinking" program at one of the nearby Missions and had come to realize that he drank when he felt bad. He drank when his anger and sadness and hurt and fear overcame him. He refused to believe that he was always going to have a drinking problem. He was determined to regain control of his life. He realized that to accomplish this he would have to deal with his emotions. He got involved with a mental health program sponsored by the city that helped him get in touch with this will power and his self-esteem. He said he began to feel like he was gonna make it back.

He told me that the greatest realization he ever had was the morning he saw his wife standing near his feet beneath the cardboard that was his shelter. He described the look on her face and peaceful and kind. He said he heard in his mind the thought that he was a better man than his behavior. He said he buried his face in his bent arms and cried for quite a while.

From that time on he moderated his drinking and eventually quit. He knew both in his head and his heart that it was bad for him. He began to seek help from charities and from city services. Slowly he was getting back on his feet.

A few days after he and I spoke he got a job at the produce market, and with his first paycheck got a room on a week-to-week basis. He was looking into other employment, but wasn't sure what he wanted to do. I knew he would find the right thing. He had a sense of determination, a positive outlook on life in general, and on his life in particular.

This man taught me that the force of will is a might and wonderful thing. He showed me that if you believe and work towards what you want to be and believe you are, you can become that being.

He wanted to change.
He believed he would change.
He worked to change.
You can change, too.

The choice is yours.

Some people have chided me for my work with the addicted, preferring to ignore the problem and hoping it will go away and be fixed by someone else.

Drugs and drink can play a role if you let them. Most of us at one time or another will have an issue to work on, and some of us choose drugs and drink as a way around the issue. Or as a way to forget the issue, the problem, for a while.

But the bottom line is this: the use of these products is not the larger issue. What is most important is the true well-being of the user.

And sometimes we forget this.

DAILY CHANGE

How we start our day has a tremendous effect on how the day fares: was it productive, did the things that had to be done get done? Did I attend to details that might otherwise blow up later? Did I waste time, either daydreaming or immobilized by my emotions? How we approach the start of the day can be noticeable to others as well, especially when they ask if we "got up on the wrong side of the bed." It happens, even to the best of us. We are still human, at least for right now. Part of transforming one's life is to start the day so that is conducive to, and sets the stage for, a good day. For years now, it has been my habit to say, "Thank you" each morning upon waking. In this small act, I thank God, or whatever, for giving me another day in which to grow and learn. I used to jangle my nerves every morning with an alarm clock that was so loud and insistent that neighbors once asked if I could set it at a more convenient time for them to awaken!

There was a time when I would shut off my alarm clock and somehow, without too much physical damage from colliding with furniture and/or walls, stumble into the kitchen to get some coffee into me so that I could wake up, or so I believed. On the mornings when the coffee wasn't there, I would grab another source of caffeine. Anything. Something.

One day a friend commented on my sleepy demeanor as I came into work. I told her I had not yet had my morning coffee. She smiled and said that she remembered being addicted to coffee and how she hated it.

As I walked away, I thought, "I'm not addicted." Then I realized that I was lying to myself. Right there I decided to lessen my reliance and dependence on caffeine to get me going in the morning, and to keep me going throughout the day. The next few mornings were memorable as I struggled to overcome my addiction. But I wanted to be in control. I didn't want to be controlled by the coffee. And the cigarette and the whole routine.

Today, I live without caffeine or cigarettes to stimulate me. I control the relationship now, not they. And while I was altering my morning routine, I learned to create a routine that was nourishing and fulfilling for me. No longer did I drag myself out of bed and stumble awake. I determined that I needed to be fully and completely in my body before I tried to use it. No more stubbing my toes or gouging myself with furniture. Why should I start my day by hurting myself? Why was I being so disrespectful of my own body, my own self? Certainly not because I loved myself.

To change my wake-up routine, I had to assess my needs. Did I need to use the bathroom first thing? If so, go. If not, then what? Turning on the TV? That was worse than the alarm clock. All of that sound and light just distracted me at its best. The few times I tried just sitting quietly with myself, kind of meditating, I fell back to sleep. Out of all the various methods and ways that I tried, the one that truly worked for me was to start with me, so to speak.

Now when I wake up, after giving thanks, I take care of any bodily needs. It is difficult to progress beyond this step and to ignore my body, because that is what I am going to be engaging next.

In a comfortable position that suits me, I now acknowledge my physical form, my shell, my body. I think of my body as my own personal time and space machine. It has carried me through time to this point, as well as around this planet. It is only right and just that I acknowledge its importance in my life. Without it, I am not here.

Starting at my feet, I take stock of myself in the physical sense. Are my feet OK? Are there any tensions I need to be aware of? I move then, flexing my toes and ankles, feeling the muscles and skin move to my mental command. If I like, I reach down and touch them, feeling the warmth of my skin and the strength of my muscles. From here I progress up my body, noting any conditions that signal any discomfort or imbalance. This is where breath work helps me.

When I have completed my "pre-flight checkout," I give thought and feeling to the kind of day I want to have. I concentrate on the positive aspects of life, which is to say the joy, the love, the compassion, the caring that I hope to express when the occasions arise. My singular goal is to be fully in each moment as it occurs, both at the time of this thought and later as I go through my day.

Next for me comes physical exercise to help keep my body in a shape that suits me. As I've gotten older I have come to truly appreciate my physical form. Not because of my ego, but perhaps in spite of it.

Next comes clothing. I dress for me now, not for someone else. I wear what I am. Today the body coverings I choose reflect who I am. I am the one wearing the clothes, and I need to be comfortable in them.

Moving on, I now come to my personal calendar for this day. I review the chores that I want to accomplish in this day, all the tasks that have nothing to do with my work day, but constitute part of my life. From this sometimes prodigious list I will choose a certain number to accomplish today, based on balancing my personal and work calendars.

Lastly comes my work calendar. This review is similar to the review of my personal calendar. It is as important, but not more so, than my personal calendar. I don't try to place more emphasis on one part of my day, but to treat it as a whole. To place all of my focus on part of my day is to diminish all of the other parts to some degree.

Now I am ready to get up and get moving. I have reviewed those things I want to accomplish in my day and I feel ready to go about it. This process of ordering my day has helped provide me with clarity.

EXERCISE THIRTEEN

Find a comfortable space where you will not be disturbed. Sit down and relax. Take several deep breaths.

Consider changing your morning routine. Examine how you start your day. Ask yourself, "What things would I like to change about how my day begins each morning?"

Implement those changes you feel would make your morning better for you. If you share your living space with others, effect a change—or changes—that would work for all concerned, without minimizing or upsetting anyone, especially yourself.

As you work toward the goal of a better morning routine, each day will help you to clarify and refine the "how" of a better start to your day.

ON THE ROAD

N ow comes the good and the fun—and maybe the hard part: continuing what you've begun.

Life is what you make it. Each and every day we are alive is a good day.

Live each day, not as your last but as your best.

You now have a semblance of your authentic self. Continuing on the path we have shared in this book will lead you to an even greater relationship with yourself and the world around you. And the better you make that relationship the better your life will be.

Thank you for taking the time and effort to "do" this workbook. It is my sincere hope that you will prosper and benefit from your investment.

Take care and be well.

If you wish, please feel free to write me at the address below:

Heikkie Dean
2370 Market Street, Box 210
San Francisco, CA 94114

Or you can contact me via the internet at Heikkie.com if you prefer.

Many people helped me in the process of making this book. Thank you all so very much. Special thanks Barbara Tetzlaff, David Lloyd, Martin Ross and Jeff Campbell. Angelic thanks to Tina Tucker. And gratitude for all that everyone has taught me.